Usborne
First Sticker Book
My Friends

Illustrated by Joanne Partis

Words by Holly Bathie

Designed by Meg Dobbie

You'll find all the stickers at the back of the book.

All kinds of friends

A friend is someone you like to spend time with.
Stick all kinds of different friends onto these pages.
Do you have a special friend?

This is my monkey, Chip.
He goes everywhere with me.

I talk to my pet lizard, Ziggy.
He listens to me patiently.

My friends live on my street and
we play together all the time.

I love my puppy, Tickle.
She's always happy to see me.

My friend Bilal is good at board games.

My brother Anil is my best friend. He's so funny.

My friends at judo club are kind. They help me learn the moves.

I like to spend time with my grandad. We grow vegetables.

My friend Eli is always smiling, but only I can see him.

At the playground

Stick on lots of friends playing together here. You can add more kind and friendly words to the yellow speech bubbles too.

Party friends

These friends are wearing their best clothes for a party. Stick on more children, then add more tasty food, balloons and presents.

At the park

It's a perfect day to be outside at the park.
Stick on more hungry ducks to feed, and
some friends kicking a ball around.

Fun at home

These children are all playing indoors today. Stick on more friends having fun together in different ways.

We fill our scrapbook with things we've found outdoors.

We learn the words to songs and sing along together.

My cousin and I both like to paint and draw.

I enjoy making a den with my brothers.

It's fun to jump and spin around, and make up dances. Jazzy the dog joins in too!

We love baking things (and then eating them).

Together, we can build tall towers.

Friends at preschool

It's a busy day at preschool. Stick on lots of things to play with, and more friends dressing up.

Visiting a farm

This farm has little lambs to feed and a big blue tractor to play on. Stick on more animals, and some friends splashing in the puddles.

Sleeping over

Aisha is staying at her friend's house. Stick on her cuddly teddy bear, and a soft night-light so she feels at home.

At the playground

Visiting a farm pages 14-15